Who Lives in the Rainforests of the World?

The world's rainforests are home to many amazing creatures! You might see a group of monkeys jumping in the treetops, a green snake curled around a branch, and a sleepy sloth snuggled up for a nap. There are spotted jaguars, scarlet macaws, giant bats, and so much more!

More than half of the world's animals live in rainforests. Many plants grow there, too, providing food and shelter for millions of insects, birds, reptiles, fish, and mammals. Different creatures thrive in each part of the rainforest, from the dark, damp forest floor to the sunny emergent layer above the tallest trees.

This poster project includes stickers of some of the wonderful creatures who live in each layer of the rainforest. Learn about the different layers as you put the creature stickers in the right place.

Make a Giant
RAINFOREST POSTER

Learn about the wonders of the rainforest by putting together a beautiful poster to hang on your wall! Use the stickers to complete the rainforest scene on the poster.

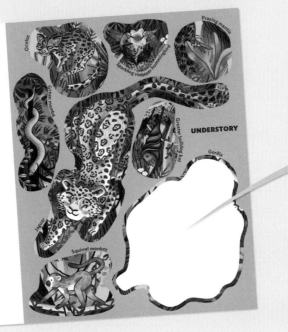

1. Unfold your poster and lay it flat on a table.

2. Pick a sticker and find the outline on the poster that matches it.

3. Place the sticker on its spot on the poster. Watch your rainforest scene come alive as you add more stickers!

4. Hang your finished poster on your wall. How many rainforest creatures can you name?

Where do CREATURES of the RAINFOREST live?

EMERGENT LAYER

Above the trees, the sun shines brightly and rain falls heavily. Small mammals move among the branches, and colorful birds and butterflies fly high above the whole forest.

- Harpy eagle
- Scarlet macaw
- Capuchin monkey
- Spider monkey
- Pygmy glider
- Flying fox
- Blue morpho butterfly

CANOPY LAYER

The tangled, leafy roof of the rainforest teems with life. Rich with fruits and seeds, it provides a home to 90 percent of animals in the rainforest! Those animals move from tree to tree by hopping, jumping, or flying.

- Toco toucan
- Canary-winged parakeet
- Green iguana
- Sun parakeet
- Chimpanzee
- Red-eyed tree frog
- Blue-and-yellow macaw
- Orchid bee
- Draco lizard
- Screaming piha
- Howler monkey
- Sloth
- Emerald tree boa

UNDERSTORY

The shady, damp understory in the middle of the rainforest is home to shorter plants and many smaller animals. Some large animals use this layer for hunting.

- Green mamba
- Jaguar
- Sparkling violetear hummingbird
- Squirrel monkey
- Greater bulldog bat
- Amazon tree boa
- Gorilla
- Praying mantis
- Firefly
- Ocelot

FOREST FLOOR

With very little sunlight, plants have a hard time growing here. But lots of insects, reptiles, and amphibians live here, along with some large animals.

- Capybara
- Leopard
- Fossa
- Hercules beetle
- Scorpion
- Goliath bird-eating tarantula
- Leafcutter ant
- Burrowing worm
- Giant anteater
- Pangolin
- Giant centipede
- Poison dart frog

RAINFOREST WATERS

Because they receive so much rainfall, rainforests have some of the largest rivers in the world. Many interesting animals make their homes in these waters.

- Giant South American river turtle
- Giant river otter
- Amazon river dolphin
- Freshwater stingray
- Amazonian manatee
- Electric eel
- Arapaima
- Piranha

NOTE: *These animals don't all live in the same rainforest. For instance, jaguars are found in South and Central America, while chimpanzees live in Africa.*

Spider monkey

Blue morpho butterfly

Capuchin monkey

Harpy eagle

Pygmy glider

Flying fox

Scarlet macaw

Blue-and-yellow macaw

Emerald tree boa

Sloth

Sun parakeet

Chimpanzee

Orchid bee

Green iguana

Red-eyed tree frog

Draco lizard

Canary-winged parakeet

Toco toucan

Howler monkey

Screaming piha

Ocelot

Sparkling violetear hummingbird

Praying mantis

Green mamba

UNDERSTORY

Greater bulldog bat

Gorilla

Jaguar

Squirrel monkey

Firefly

Amazon tree boa

Goliath bird-eating tarantula

Giant centipede

FOREST FLOOR

Pangolin

Poison dart frog

Capybara

Scorpion

Fossa

Hercules beetle

Leafcutter ant

Giant anteater

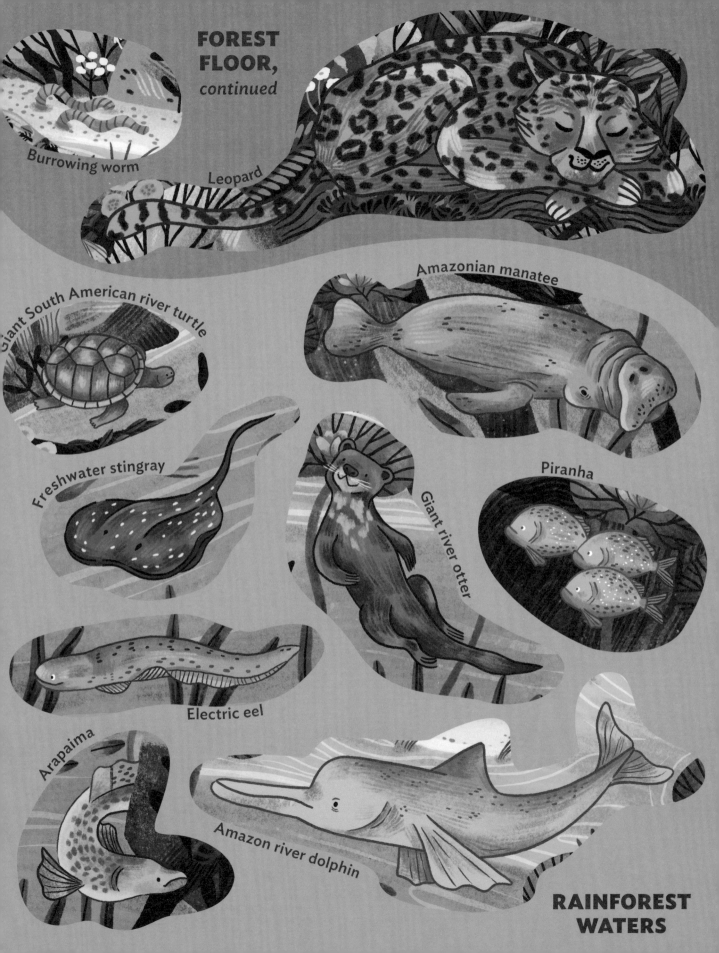

Burrowing worm

Leopard

Giant South American river turtle

Amazonian manatee

Freshwater stingray

Giant river otter

Piranha

Electric eel

Arapaima

Amazon river dolphin

RAINFOREST WATERS